JAGUAR

NORTH AMERICA'S BIGGEST BEASTS

Elizabeth Morgan

PowerKiDS
press

New York

Published in 2016 by The Rosen Publishing Group, Inc.
29 East 21st Street, New York, NY 10010

First Edition

Editor: Katie Kawa
Book Design: Reann Nye

Photo Credits: Cover (background) Galyna Andrushko/Shutterstock.com; cover (jaguar), p. 1 bluehand/Shutterstock.com; p. 4 Pashin Georgiy/Shutterstock.com; p. 5 Volt Collection/Shutterstock.com; p. 6 © iStockphpoto.com/Alexander Bedrin; pp. 7 (background), 11 (background) worldswildlifewonders/Shutterstockcom; p. 7 (jaguar) Pal Teravagimov/Shutterstock.com; p. 7 (snow leopard) KateChris/Shutterstock.com; p. 7 (tiger) Eduard Kyslynskyy/Shutterstock.com; p. 7 (lion) Maggy Meyer/Shutterstock.com; p. 7 (leopard) GUDKOV ANDREY/Shutterstock.com; p. 8 Ian Rentoul/Shutterstock.com; p. 9 ANDRE DIB/Shutterstock.com; p. 10 Photo by James Keith/Moment Open/Getty Images; p. 11 (capybara) Vadim Petrakov/Shutterstock.com; p. 11 (tapir) Andrea Izzotti/Shutterstock.com; p. 11 (turtle) Celiafoto/Shutterstock.com; pp. 12–13 Steve Winter/National Geographic/Getty Images; p. 14 Shchipkova Elena/Shutterstock.com; p. 15 Jeff Foott/Discovery Channel Images/Getty Images; p. 16 D. DAVIDS/DAVIDS/WireImages/Getty Images; pp. 17, 18 Kris Wiktor/Shutterstock.com; p. 19 FCG/Shutterstock.com; p. 20 Juriah Mosin/Shutterstock.com; p. 21 milosk50/Shutterstock.com; p. 22 Ammit Jack/Shutterstock.com.

Cataloging-in-Publication Data

Morgan, Elizabeth.
Jaguar / by Elizabeth Morgan.
p. cm. — (North America's biggest beasts)
Includes index.
ISBN 978-1-5081-4303-1 (pbk.)
ISBN 978-1-5081-4304-8 (6-pack)
ISBN 978-1-5081-4305-5 (library binding)
1. Jaguar — Juvenile literature. I. Morgan, Elizabeth. II. Title.
QL737.C23 M675 2016
599.755—d23

Manufactured in the United States of America

CPSIA Compliance Information: Batch #BW16PK: For Further Information contact Rosen Publishing, New York, New York at 1-800-237-9932

CONTENTS

Cool Cats

Cats are common throughout North America—from tiny house cats to massive mountain lions. However, one of these cats is bigger than any other in North America or South America. It's the jaguar!

Jaguars are the largest cats in the Western Hemisphere, which is the half of Earth where North America is located. A jaguar's big, strong body makes it a powerful predator. In fact, the name "jaguar" comes from the Native American word *yaguar*, which means "he who kills with one leap." Read on to learn more about these cool cats!

house cat

It's hard to believe that huge jaguars and small house cats are **related**—but it's true!

Roaring with the Big Cats

Jaguars have a long body built for hunting. A jaguar's body is generally between 5 and 6 feet (1.5 and 1.8 m) long. In addition, it has a tail that can be up to 3 feet (0.9 m) long! The average weight of a jaguar is around 220 pounds (99.8 kg).

Jaguars are part of a group of cats known as big cats. The scientific name for this group is *Panthera*. Cats in this group are known for their ability to roar, and they're the only cats that can make this sound.

THE BIG IDEA

Jaguars are the only cats in the group *Panthera* that are found in the wild in either North America or South America.

COMPARING BIG CATS

NAME		BODY LENGTH (NOT INCLUDING TAIL)	WEIGHT
Siberian tiger (largest kind of tiger)	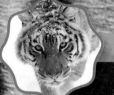	at least **10.75 feet** **(3.3 m)**	**660 pounds** **(299.4 kg)**
lion		**4.5 to 6.5 feet** **(1.4 to 2 m)**	**265 to 420 pounds** **(120.2 to 190.5 kg)**
jaguar		**5 to 6 feet** **(1.5 to 1.8 m)**	average of **220 pounds** **(99.8 kg)**
leopard		**4.25 to 6.25 feet** **(1.3 to 1.9 m)**	**66 to 176 pounds** **(29.9 to 79.8 kg)**
snow leopard		**4 to 5 feet** **(1.2 to 1.5 m)**	**60 to 120 pounds** **(27.2 to 54.4 kg)**

The group of big, roaring cats known as *Panthera* is made up of tigers, lions, jaguars, leopards, and snow leopards. Although snow leopards are generally considered part of this group, they actually can't roar.

Strength and Spots

A jaguar is built for hunting for more reasons than just its powerful size. It also has a very strong **jaw**, which it uses to attack its **prey**. Its jaw is strong enough to bite through the top of a turtle's shell!

A jaguar's spots also help it hunt. A jaguar is orange or tan with black spots. These spots are called "rosettes" because they're shaped like little roses. The spots help it blend in with its surroundings in order to kill its prey with a surprise attack.

THE BIG IDEA

Some jaguars are so dark that it looks as if they don't have any spots. However, these jaguars still have spots. They're just harder to see on the jaguar's dark coat.

Jaguars are known for their beautiful, spotted coat.
In fact, some people hunt jaguars for their fur.

On the Hunt

Jaguars are carnivores, which means they only eat meat. The ability to surprise prey is very important for jaguars. They hide in forests and sometimes in trees as they wait for prey to walk by. Then, they **pounce**!

Jaguars can kill their prey with one bite. Often, they bite the back of an animal's **skull**, which kills it immediately. Jaguars have strong teeth to deliver such a deadly bite. Then, jaguars drag their prey to a hidden spot to eat it.

THE BIG IDEA

Jaguars are strong swimmers. They hunt fish and turtles that live in rivers and streams.

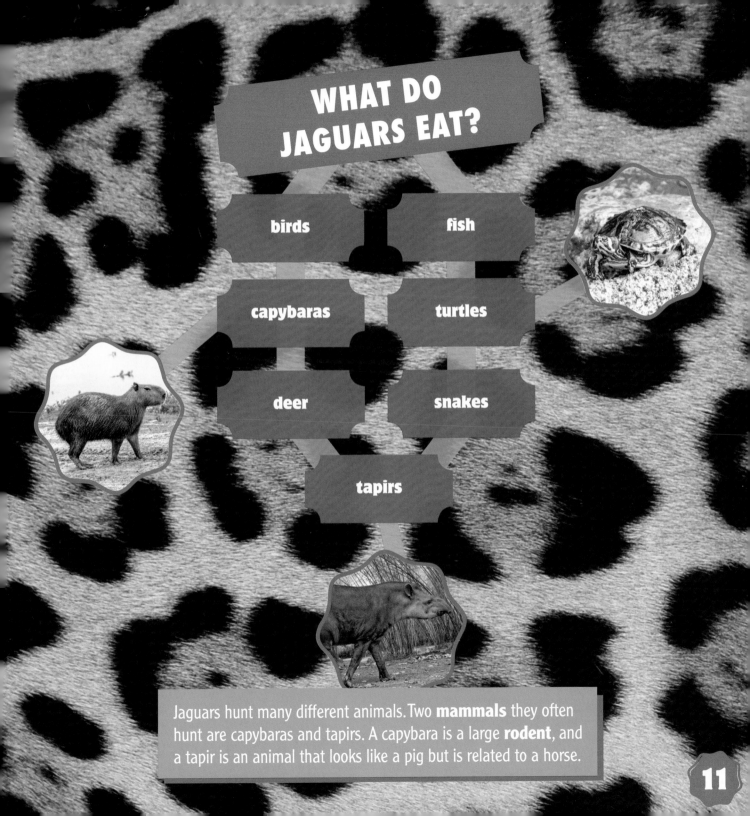

WHAT DO JAGUARS EAT?

birds

fish

capybaras

turtles

deer

snakes

tapirs

Jaguars hunt many different animals. Two **mammals** they often hunt are capybaras and tapirs. A capybara is a large **rodent**, and a tapir is an animal that looks like a pig but is related to a horse.

North American Jaguars

Having plenty of places to hide is very important for jaguars. This is why they're often found in wooded areas and tropical—or hot and wet—forests. Many jaguars also live near rivers, streams, or **swamps**.

Jaguars once lived over a much larger **range** that extended from the southern United States to the tip of South America. However, they're now found mainly in South America and the southern part of North America, which is called Central America. A small number of jaguars still live in the southwestern United States.

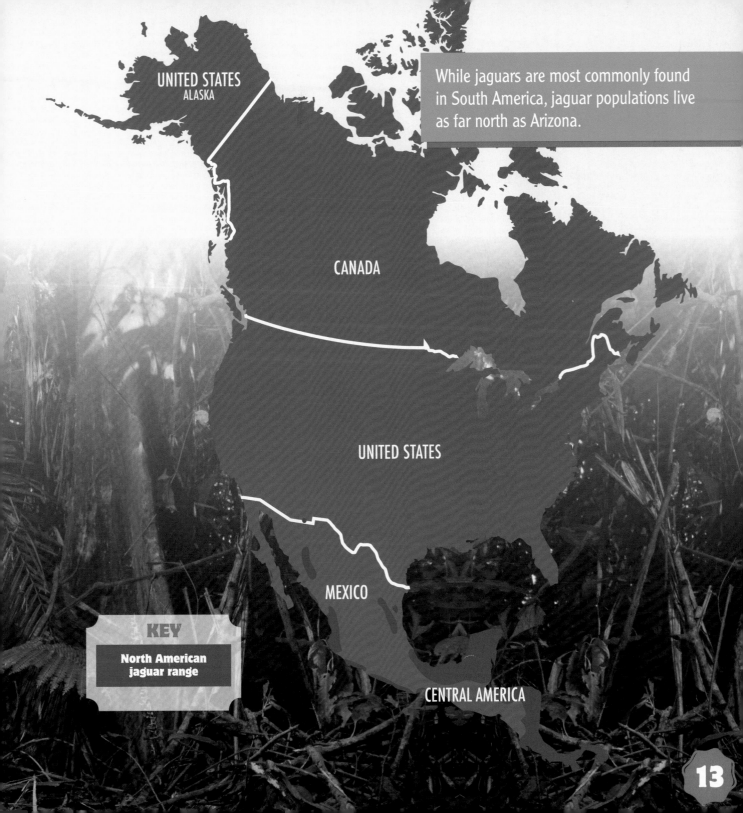

While jaguars are most commonly found in South America, jaguar populations live as far north as Arizona.

UNITED STATES
ALASKA

CANADA

UNITED STATES

MEXICO

CENTRAL AMERICA

KEY

North American
jaguar range

13

Home on the Range

Within their larger range, jaguars have their own separate home ranges. These are areas where a jaguar lives and hunts. Jaguars are solitary animals, which means they generally live alone.

Jaguars mark their home ranges in different ways, so other jaguars know not to make their home there. They scratch trees on the edge of the range with their claws. They also leave bodily waste around the range, and the sight and smell tell other jaguars—as well as other animals or people—to stay away.

A jaguar's home range is also called its territory. This jaguar is marking its territory by leaving claw marks on a tree trunk.

15

Baby Jaguars

The only time jaguars aren't solitary is during the mating season. This is the time when jaguars come together to mate, or make babies. Female jaguars that are ready to mate call to male jaguars. The males then answer with their own calls.

Female jaguars give birth to one to four babies at a time. The babies are born with their eyes closed and can't see for up to two weeks. They stay with their mother for around two years as they learn to hunt.

THE BIG IDEA

Baby jaguars are called cubs.

Female jaguars won't let any other animal near their cubs. This includes male jaguars!

Hiding from Humans

Jaguars are such feared predators that most other animals won't attack them. However, people in North America and South America hunt these big beasts. A jaguar's size and strength are no match for hunters with guns.

Jaguars use the same tricks to hide from people as they do to surprise their prey. Their spots allow them to stay hidden in forests, making it hard for hunters to find them. If a hunter does corner a jaguar, the jaguar could attack with its sharp claws or teeth.

Jaguars are great at hiding in the forest. This helps them when they're acting as hunters and when people are hunting them.

19

An Endangered Animal

Hunters sell jaguar teeth and even jaguar paws, but they especially want to sell jaguar fur. In most countries, it's illegal to hunt jaguars for any reason. Jaguars are considered an endangered species in the United States. This means they're at risk of dying out.

Jaguars also face other dangers posed by people besides hunting for **profit**. Building projects take away their **habitats**. Also, jaguars have been known to eat animals, such as cows, that live on ranches. When this happens, ranchers sometimes kill jaguars to keep them from eating any more livestock.

THE BIG IDEA

Jaguars can live around 12 years in the wild. Jaguars living in zoos or other places where people care for them can live over 20 years.

Laws have been passed in most countries, including the United States, to stop jaguar hunting. However, some people break these laws and continue to hunt jaguars illegally, which is also known as poaching.

Nothing Else Like It!

Hunting and habitat loss are a big part of the reason why the jaguar's range has shrunk so much over the years. However, people are working to keep these endangered animals around for many years to come. By learning more about these big cats and where they live, people can become more aware of the ways we can keep them safe.

Jaguars are big, beautiful animals with a powerful body built for hunting. There's no other animal in North America like the jaguar!

Glossary

habitat: The natural home for plants, animals, and other living things.

jaw: Either of the two bony parts of the face where teeth grow.

mammal: Any warm-blooded animal whose babies drink milk and whose body is covered with hair or fur.

pounce: To suddenly attack something with the intent of taking it.

prey: An animal hunted by other animals for food.

profit: Money that is made.

range: The open area of land over which animals move and feed.

related: Belonging to the same group or family because of shared qualities.

rodent: A small animal, such as a mouse, rat, or beaver, that has sharp front teeth.

skull: The bones that form the head and face of a person or animal.

swamp: Land that is always wet and often partly covered with water.

Index

Websites

Due to the changing nature of Internet links, PowerKids Press has developed an online list of websites related to the subject of this book. This site is updated regularly. Please use this link to access the list: www.powerkidslinks.com/nabb/jagr